SIX DAYS
of
CREATION

HENRY M. MORRIS III

Dallas, Texas
www.icr.org

Dr. Henry M. Morris III holds four earned degrees, including a D.Min. from Luther Rice Seminary and the Presidents and Key Executives MBA from Pepperdine University. A former college professor, administrator, business executive, and senior pastor, Dr. Morris is an articulate and passionate speaker frequently invited to address church congregations, college assemblies, and national conferences. The eldest son of ICR's founder, Dr. Morris has served for many years in conference and writing ministry. His love for the Word of God and passion for Christian maturity, coupled with God's gift of teaching, have given Dr. Morris a broad and effective ministry over the years. He has authored numerous articles and books, including *The Big Three: Major Events that Changed History Forever; Exploring the Evidence for Creation; 5 Reasons to Believe in Recent Creation; The Book of Beginnings, Vol. 1: Creation, Fall, and the First Age; The Book of Beginnings, Vol. 2: Noah, the Flood, and the New World; The Book of Beginnings, Vol. 3: The Patriarchs, a Promised Nation, and the Dawning of the Second Age; Pulling Down Strongholds: Achieving Spiritual Victory through Strategic Offense; A Firm Foundation: Devotional Insights to Help You Know, Believe, and Defend Truth; Six Days of Creation;* and *Your Origins Matter.*

SIX DAYS OF CREATION
by Henry M. Morris III, D.Min.

First printing: February 2013
Second printing: April 2013
Third printing: September 2014

All Scripture quotations are from the New King James Version.

ISBN: 978-1-935587-18-7

Please visit our website for other books and resources: www.icr.org

Printed in the United States of America.

TABLE OF CONTENTS

INTRODUCTION

> In the beginning God created the heavens and the earth.
> (Genesis 1:1)

Everybody believes in something. Whether secular humanist, atheist, ardent Muslim, or other belief, all men and women have faith in something—some "source" that expresses their beliefs about who they are and why they are here.

The book of Genesis is the source for the Christian belief system. It is the foundation of everything that God has undertaken on behalf of humanity. For that reason, a correct understanding of Genesis is essential for a correct understanding of our identity, our responsibility, and our future.

Genesis presents an all-powerful and all-knowing Creator, transcendent to the universe, the First Cause who spoke all things into existence. Some Christian leaders and teachers, however, would not agree that God created the universe "out of nothing" during the creation event. Others have suggested that God was merely involved in the background, or somehow operated through natural forces to eventually produce the organized and functioning structures of nature.

The biblical text, however, is consistent in its record that there were omnipotent and omniscient acts of creation. The Scriptures also agree that during the creation week God *made* and *shaped* that which He had *created* into an organized and functioning *cosmos*, which "was very good"

(Genesis 1:31). Those who reject Genesis 1:1—who deny that God created anything at all—have by every means possible sought to disprove this fact. Darwinian evolution has as its chief presupposition a disbelief in God and creation. The very idea of an omnipotent, omniscient Supreme Being is anathema to naturalistic concepts of existence.

Interestingly, the academic world has begun to entertain "spiritual" interpretations of naturalistic science as the evidence for complexity and design grows more and more obvious. Yet most academics still cling to evolutionary cosmologies because they cannot accept an omnipotent and omniscient Creator.

Handling the actual texts of Scripture, then, becomes fundamentally important. Should we believe in a literal creation? Are the written words of the book of Genesis to be treated as historical fact? What does Genesis have to say about what and how God created?

The answers to these questions are vital not only to our understanding of origins, but to our understanding of God Himself.

∾ 1 ∾
DAY ONE

In the beginning God created the heavens and the earth. The earth was without form, and void; and darkness was on the face of the deep. And the Spirit of God was hovering over the face of the waters. (Genesis 1:1-2)

Genesis 1 is not difficult to understand. Its grammatical structure clearly falls within the *narrative* genre; in other words, it is a historical account. God created the world and all it contains in six 24-hour days. When God Himself refers to this creation event in Exodus 20:11, He insists that Genesis 1 is to be taken as the prototype for a six-day work week. There is no ambiguity. Only those who do not want to accept Genesis as real history refuse to recognize that.

Three Key Verbs

Genesis was originally written in the Hebrew language, and it is helpful to understand key Hebrew terms used in the creation account.

- *Bārāʾ* means to create, shape, or fashion. It is used when God creates the heavens and the earth, the animals, and man.

- *ʾAsah* means to do, fashion, accomplish, make, etc. It is used when God constructs something (such as stars) from elements He previously created.

- *Yatsar* means to form, fashion, shape, or sculpt. It implies a "hands-on" involvement, and is used to describe God forming beasts and birds out of the ground and man out of the dust.

People can fashion or make things, but only God can "create" (*bārā*). He created *ex nihilo* (out of nothing) everything that currently exists. Genesis 1:1 establishes the triune nature of the universe—in the beginning (time) God created the heavens (space) and the earth (matter). The earth is described as "without form" and "void." Proponents of the gap theory usually translate these words as "ruined" and "desolate," as though a cataclysmic event had happened after the initial creation. But the more straightforward reading of the text is that God created the heavens and the earth in their basic elemental components, and these were without form and empty, waiting to be developed by God.

The Development of the Universe Begins

God's next step was to start the processes that make the universe function—energy, gravity, etc. The text states that the third Person of the Trinity, the Holy Spirit, was "hovering" over the waters, a word that can easily be understood as "vibrating" or "fluttering." The work of the Holy Spirit in creation on Day One was to energize the earth in order to prepare it for the rest of the creation events.

> Then God said, "Let there be light"; and there was light. And God saw the light, that it was good; and God divided the light from the darkness. God called the light Day, and the darkness He called Night. So the evening and the morning were the first day. (Genesis 1:3-5)

The biblical record indicates that God separated the light from the darkness. This most likely indicates that the earth of Day One was shaped into a sphere (by the Holy Spirit "energizing" it). The words that follow confirm this fact, for God concludes Day One with "the evening and the morning were the first day." A definite system of time had been developed, a dark-light cycle, which man observes today in the rotation of the earth, allowing light during the "morning" and darkness during the "evening."

It is worth noting that at the very beginning, God used a specific linguistic structure to define what He was doing. There was a "light" portion, which God named "day," and a "dark" portion, which God named "night." This sequence of "evening and morning" was specifically called the first day (Genesis 1:5). That same linguistic formula is repeated throughout the following sequence of night-day cycles, reinforcing both the specificity of the phenomena and the time-motion regularity of the process as literal, 24-hour days.

The Tri-Universe and the Nature of God

As would be expected in any product by an intelligent being, the product (in this case the universe itself) would give some insight into the nature of the originator. According to the Bible, God imprinted something about Himself in the things that He created and made, so that all of humanity would be able to "clearly see" His invisible attributes, even His "eternal power and Godhead" (Romans 1:20).

The biblical concept of the Trinity is very difficult to understand. Many physical illustrations have been offered (an egg, a triangle, etc.), but all of these are *triads*. They are composed of parts that collected together make a different whole, but that are easily separated into individual components. A triad can also be seen as a phased sequence (e.g., liquid, gas, solid) that can only exist in one form at a time. A *trinity*, although composed of three different things, cannot be separated or disconnected in any way from each "piece" of the whole.

Thus, the more precise illustration of God's triune nature is the universe that God Himself created. It is a "uni-verse," one thing containing separately definable and distinguishable entities (space-matter-time) that cannot be taken apart.

Space itself is a trinity. We can conceive of it as height, depth, and length, but we cannot capture or eliminate it in any way. Space is not "nothing," but we are unable to discover fully what it is. Space exists *in* all things—and all things have their existence in space. Nothing exists outside of space, except the Creator Himself and that which is created to transcend the creation by the Creator's design.

Matter is also a trinity—energy (matter generated), motion (matter manifested), and phenomena (matter experienced). As scientists learn more about the nature of matter (mass-energy), they have discovered that everything is a phenomenon of unique energy in motion, patterns and structure (e.g., molecules), and processes (e.g., motion, metabolism, etc.). Essentially, invisible space is understood by the presence of matter in it.

Time is the third element of the tri-unity of the universe: generated in the future, flowing through the present, and into the past. We cannot understand or control time. We can only experience it. All things that exist are "experienced" through and by time. Space itself is experienced in time. Matter is only revealed as the motion that its energy manifests during time. Time cannot be separated or removed from any of the universe.

In Genesis 1:1, the Hebrew for "God" is *Elohim*, a plural noun, yet normally represented by a singular pronoun "He." This is the first foreshadowing of the marvelous doctrine of the Trinity—only one Creator God, yet functioning as three divine Persons. It is significant that His created universe is actually a tri-universe, with each of its distinct components (space-matter-time) comprising and pervading the whole universe.

God the Father is like the space of the universe: the Source and Background of all things. God the Son is like the matter (mass-energy) of the universe: the Visible One and Revealer of the Godhead. God the Spirit is like the time of the universe: the One who makes it possible to experience the work and will of God.

The Father planned the work of creation, the Son did the work ("all things were made by Him"—John 1:3), and the Spirit energized it ("the Spirit of God moved"). The Triune God created and now sustains our tri-universe!

～2～
DAY TWO

Then God said, "Let there be a firmament in the midst of the waters, and let it divide the waters from the waters." Thus God made the firmament, and divided the waters which were under the firmament from the waters which were above the firmament; and it was so. And God called the firmament Heaven. So the evening and the morning were the second day. (Genesis 1:6-8)

Once the initial universe was created by the will and purpose of God (Revelation 4:11), the triune Godhead now began "making" and "shaping" the heavens and the earth into an organized and functioning *cosmos* in preparation for the life that would be created on Days Five and Six.

The Firmament

Day Two of creation involved the making (*'asah*) of the "firmament" and the "dividing" of the waters. "Firmament" comes from the Hebrew *raqiya* and is usually translated "expanse" in more recent Bible versions. The Hebrew term clearly means an "extended surface" or a "thin, stretched-out space." This *raqiya* is inserted in the "waters," causing them to be divided. Some of these waters were to be situated above the *raqiya*, with the remainder staying below. Peter speaks of "the earth standing out of water and in the water" (2 Peter 3:5), and the prophet Isaiah reveals to us that as God sat above the circle of the earth, He "stretches out the heavens like a curtain, and spreads them out like a tent to dwell in" (Isaiah 40:22).

Elsewhere in the Old Testament, *raqiya* is often used to describe different "expanses." The "speech" and "knowledge" of the Creator are openly declared in the "firmament" (Psalm 19:1-2). Ezekiel describes a "firmament" above the heads of the cherubim that was like a "sapphire" supporting the throne of God (Ezekiel 1:26; 10:1). Daniel tells us that the wise will shine like the "brightness of the firmament" and the "stars" (Daniel 12:3). Obviously, the Hebrew term is meant to be descriptive rather than nominative. *Raqiya* is a "thing" that God made, but it is more often used as an adjective to describe how it is used. Perhaps that is why God specifically named the *raqiya* "heaven" (Genesis 1:8).

While the specific naming of the "expanse" is designated as "heaven" during the activity of the second day, the Old Testament uses the proper name "heaven" over 400 times and in several different ways.

- It is used of both the solar system and the starry universe when God describes the "lights" that He develops on Day Four (Genesis 1:14-17). This broad and inclusive use is common, both in our normal speech and in the Old Testament.

- It is used of the atmosphere in which the birds are to fly "above the earth across the face of the firmament of the heavens" (Genesis 1:20). The birds "of the air" are mentioned an additional 16 times in the Old Testament.

- It is used by God Himself during His discourse with Job to describe the stars and galaxies of the universe: "Can you bind the cluster of the Pleiades, Or loose the belt of Orion? Can you bring out Mazzaroth in its season? Or can you guide the Great Bear with its cubs? Do you know the ordinances of the heavens? Can you set their dominion over the earth?" (Job 38:31-33).

- It is also used specifically of the sun and moon (our near solar system). "Then Joshua spoke to the LORD…'Sun, stand still over Gibeon; And Moon, in the Valley of Aijalon.'…So the sun stood still in the midst of heaven" (Joshua 10:12-13).

The Waters Above

Whatever physical properties may have been described by the information that God provides about Day Two, it is clear the upper "waters" would have been invisible to earth's inhabitants. The sun, moon, and stars would later become time references that would necessitate visibility from earth's surface. Those "waters" that remained below would eventually become "seas." In between, in the *raqiya*, all the elements necessary to sustain the "breath of life" would be formed and maintained.

What kind of water would God have placed above this expanse? Whatever it was, it would not have consisted of clouds or mist or fog; these all have droplets of water that obscure light. Nor could it have been some form of ice band in the upper reaches of the earth's "heaven," since such a barrier would either obscure the sun or be melted by it. Some have suggested that the "waters" were diffused to the outer rim of the universe itself, thus placing them beyond the sun, moon, and stars. Still others have postulated that the upper "waters" were dispersed through space in some form of "dark matter."

In addition, there is an implication that the hydrological cycle as we know it today (rain, evaporation, rain) was not functioning then, but that some sort of "mist" system watered the ground (Genesis 2:5-6). If those biblical hints are to be taken at face value, then the most likely explanation seems to be a spherical band of "waters" surrounding the earth's atmosphere. A blanket of water vapor in the ionosphere, for instance, would be quite invisible and not obstruct the light of the heavenly bodies.

Obviously, none of us really knows. We are faced with the biblical information that this first cosmos was "standing out of water and in the water" and that this unique condition "perished" under the awful cataclysm of the global Flood (2 Peter 3:5-6). That biblical scenario is verified by all of our modern scientific observations—to the extent that there is no such "water" above anywhere now, nor could atmospheric conditions as we now know them ever rain for "forty days and forty nights" as they did at the start of the Flood. Either conditions were very different in the past, as the Bible suggests, or the Bible is simply wrong. There is no in-between on this issue.

It does appear, however, that the earth *was* very different in the past. The fossil record provides evidence of a vastly different climate and ecological distribution than we observe today. Studies have indicated that the total biomass in the past (i.e., the total of all the carbon-based systems) was nearly 100 times greater than we can account for today. Coal accumulations are huge, indicating caches of plant material crushed together in seams spanning hundreds of miles. Antarctica contains one of the largest coal deposits in the world. There are billions of fish fossils massed both in depth and distribution over the entire planet. Fossil graveyards (many millions of bones) are scrambled and mingled in enormous deposits. Many fossils of plants and animals are much larger than their comparative specimens alive today (ferns and trees, squids and sharks, cockroaches and dragonflies, alligators and dinosaurs, stegodons and sloths, etc.)—the list is both amazing and a bit frightening.

Earth's catastrophic past is well-documented. Just what caused that different past is not known scientifically, but the biblical model for "waters above the firmament" suggests an intellectually plausible description of an environmental structure that would be sufficient, physically, to produce the fossil abnormalities that we know about, as well as provide for the biblical information about pre-Flood human longevity. Whatever or however the "waters" were distributed above the earth's surface, they would have produced several effects in the past that we do not observe today.

- There would have been a greenhouse effect. Wide distribution of tropical plants (ferns, palm trees, etc.) and cold-blooded animals (e.g., reptiles) would have been aided by a worldwide distribution and diffusion of the sun's energy. Today, the earth's habitable zone is quite small compared to its total surface. Something redistributed the energy/heat from the sun differently than what we observe today.

- A shield of "waters" would have resulted in a filtering of radioactive waves and particles from space. If such a band were interposed between the sun and the earth—even between the solar system and the outer universe—the shield impact would have been significant.

- A reduction in air currents (and the resulting storms) would have followed some sort of water shield above the atmosphere. Such air currents are caused by temperature differences over large areas. If the earth were largely subtropical in the past (as appears from the fossil record), then there would have been far fewer cyclonic and disastrous environmental forces at work.

- There would have been an absence of deserts and polar caps. Evidence abounds that the modern deserts and polar ice are "new" to the planet's history—in other words, they are very recent. Ruins of cities are well known, as are "stories" of disappearing ecological histories. What is available to our observation today verifies that our earth was very different not so very long ago.

- The Bible records a longevity of life in the pre-Flood world that is not experienced today. What little we know about aging indicates that our cellular disintegration is hastened by exposure to both the radiation of the sun and the extremes of climate.

Modern physics has difficulty modeling how any form of water band would have been constructed. There are difficulties with the weight of such a band of water above the near atmosphere, and problems with the energy distribution—both that which would be necessary to maintain it and that which would be required to keep the "waters" in a vapor form. Therefore, many creationists struggle with a scientific understanding of just what these "waters above the firmament" were.

Whatever they were, they are not here now (2 Peter 3:6). Nonetheless, the Bible clearly insists that the "waters" were "divided" on the second day, and in so doing, the structure of the universe and the watery matrix of Day One were forever altered.

Whatever was done during that second day, the new structure was sufficient to provide a foundation for a cosmos that was to support vast biological processes. The evening-morning cycle continued to work, and the "making" of the third day began.

∾ 3 ∾
DAY THREE

Then God said, "Let the waters under the heavens be gathered together into one place, and let the dry land appear"; and it was so. And God called the dry land Earth, and the gathering together of the waters He called Seas. And God saw that it was good. (Genesis 1:9-10)

Gathering the Waters Together

Until the organization of both the "waters under the heavens" and the "dry land," there is no evidence either in science or in the text of Scripture to suggest that the original nature of the stuff of creation was anything more than a "formless and empty" blob. The third day began with organizational processes acting on the rotating sphere that had been set in motion on the first day and divided into separate "waters" on the second day. Now, on Day Three, the earth begins to take shape.

There a few side issues worth noting here.

- Gravity is still something of a mystery to science. We know that the "force" of gravity is proportional to the "mass" (size and density) of a given structure (planet, star, etc.). But we do not know how gravity is formed, maintained, or even what it consists of.

- Magnetic fields are not the same as gravity. Magnetic fields have "poles" (north and south, positive and negative); gravity is different. Magnetic fields seem to be related to differential movement, current through a wire, directional movements of molten rock, lag time between the earth's core and its surface rotation, etc. But we still don't know how these processes started.

- Circular motion tends to throw particles away from the center of the motion—unless the particles are "contained" by a barrier of some kind (think water in a bucket being whirled around by a kid in a science project).

There are some fundamental problems here. The rotation of the earth would seem to fling the material of the earth out into space. Of course, gravity probably holds it together, but what happened to initialize that balance? The earth's magnetic field (which has nothing to do with gravity) seems to be dependent on the rotational motion of the earth. What keeps the earth at a constant speed? How do we begin to understand the most basic of these questions when we can only measure the effects?

One of the basic mysteries about the nature of matter is that the various energies involved are somewhat contradictory. This is especially true at the macro level (gravity, orbits of solar system bodies, stars, galaxies, etc.). Theories abound, and many mathematical models are used to demonstrate the current status of our thinking, but we don't *know.*

How can our planet remain suspended in space on "nothing," as described in Job 26:7? What holds the earth's "foundations" together (Psalm 104:5)? How can the incessant tides and actions of the oceans not destroy the land surfaces, and how do the continents remain in place (Jeremiah 5:22)? What keeps the star configurations so precise and regular (Job 38:31-33)? What, in fact, holds everything together, and why doesn't the universe simply explode, implode, or collapse?

Enormous energies are involved in maintaining the rotation of our earth. Gravity's unfathomable force appears to keep the earth from being torn apart by the very forces that keep "evening and morning" going. Those isolated concerns of our planet are compounded by the enormity of the intertwined complexity of the universe. Astronomers and physicists speculate about these issues, but scientifically there is no testable answer to these huge questions except the simple biblical answers that an omnipotent and omniscient Creator designed and made "the worlds" that way, and that everything is now held together by the same authority and power that created it in the first place (Colossians 1:17; Hebrews 1:3).

In One Place

The third day involved huge organizational forces of the watery matrix, coalescing the "seas" into structured water resource systems.

The biblical phrase is: "Let the waters under the heavens be gathered together into *one place* [emphasis mine]…and the gathering together of the waters He called Seas." That condition does not exist today. The earth's oceans are spread over many places, with residues of large inland lakes and river drainage systems that bear very little resemblance to the biblical descriptions of that First Age. Not only were the waters/ seas "gathered" in one place, but there were "fountains of the deep" established sometime during this process, as well as a vast water spring that was the source for four major rivers.

> Now a river went out of Eden to water the garden, and from there it parted and became four riverheads. (Genesis 2:10)

> In the six hundredth year of Noah's life, in the second month, the seventeenth day of the month, on that day all the fountains of the great deep were broken up, and the windows of heaven were opened. (Genesis 7:11)

While these references are just pieces of the picture, they do give some biblical insight to the structure of that first creation cosmology. The Bible, in several places, indicates that the universe and the earth that God initially brought into existence were quite different from what we experience now.

Earth and Its Produce

> Then God said, "Let the earth bring forth grass, the herb that yields seed, and the fruit tree that yields fruit according to its kind, whose seed is in itself, on the earth"; and it was so. And the earth brought forth grass, the herb that yields seed according to its kind, and the tree that yields fruit, whose seed is in itself according to its kind. And God

saw that it was good. So the evening and the morning were the third day. (Genesis 1:11-13)

One of the more prevalent theories today is that biological systems developed over long ages by natural processes. The Bible seems to lump all of plant science into one day's event. How could that be?

The narrative language uses specific Hebrew terms. After the water was "gathered together" and the "dry land" appeared, the earth was told (ordered by the Creator) to "bring forth!" Many modern translations use such terms as "sprout" or "produce" when converting the Hebrew phrase. The Bible paraphrase *The Message* renders the command "Earth, green up!" Maybe that's a bit of poetic license, but the literal representation of the words would be very similar: "Then God said, 'Earth, grow (sprout, produce) grass!'" The text records that the earth did indeed produce a threefold category of its "produce."

- Grass – essentially all ground-covering vegetation
- Herbs – would apply to all bushes and shrubs
- Trees – probably includes all large woody plants

Please remember that the Bible later specifically designates these earth products as "food" for the living creatures that were to populate the planet (Genesis 1:30). In no place in the Scriptures are plants ascribed the "life" that "living" creatures possess. Plants are food. They do not possess the life of animals and man. They are, indeed, marvelous and beautiful and complex and able to reproduce "after their kind," but they are designed by the Creator to be a source of energy to maintain life—they are *not* alive in the biblical sense.

Plants Are Not Simple

There is no hint anywhere, either in science or in the Scripture, that reproducing plants are the same as "earth" (dirt). There is a vast difference between dirt and grass, for instance, and the stunning molecular makeup of reproducing biology is logarithmically beyond the molecular simplicity of dirt and rock. The complexity of cellular structure and exceedingly sophisticated energy conversion mechanisms like photosynthesis far surpass the soil in which most earth "produce" lives out its cycle.

To begin with, none of the dirt formations reproduce. Some "grow" (crystals, stalactites, stalagmites, etc.), but they do not adapt to environmental changes as reproductive plants can and do. Rocks don't rock—they sit still for a very long time. Plants rock! They sway to the wind, they move in relationship to the sun, they even respond to sounds and atmospheric pressure. Rocks can be pretty, but plants are beautiful. The Lord Jesus said that even the most wealthy and glorious king who has ever lived was not clothed like the lilies of the field (Luke 12:27).

After Its Kind

God introduces a phrase on Day Three that is used ten times in Genesis 1, an additional seven times speaking of the animals at the time of Noah's Flood, and another 13 times in Leviticus and Deuteronomy defining the specific types of animal sacrifices and flesh that was suitable to eat. Evidently, the concept is important.

All of the plants of the third day were to have "seed" imbedded within the very nature of the plant itself, and all of the subsequent "yielding" of that seed (reproduction) was to be "according to its kind." Everything we know about plant biology verifies this simple statement. The biological structure and nature of any earth "product" are contained within the cellular information of that specific plant. That very complex internal information assures us that an apple tree will not produce kumquats, and that a rose (however broadly expressed) will never become a petunia.

> "For every tree is known by its own fruit. For men do not gather figs from thorns, nor do they gather grapes from a bramble bush." (Luke 6:44)

Not everybody agrees about just what the Hebrew word for "kind" (*min*) means. Its biblical use is mostly applied to living things, everything from grasshoppers to cattle. It probably is not limited to our biological term "species." It could apply to genus, or perhaps to family, but scientific studies are complex and have not yet provided enough precise information to determine with any certainty where *min* begins or ends.

However, one thing is sure: There is absolutely no proof of a common ancestor to all living things. What is absolutely certain, as far as observation is concerned, is that every plant and every animal reproduces only "after its kind." Each has its own DNA that can only direct the reproduction of the same kind. There is no indication that a fish can become a duck or that algae can become a cow—none. The informational changes are so vast that no amount of random mutations could ever innovate the necessary structural changes to the cellular data.

Written in the informational instructions of every reproductive kind are multiple "languages" for unique needs, backup systems, timing increments, master "blueprints," and cross-checks that verify the proper "connections." The more we discover about these genetic instructions, the more complex and "design intensive" the information becomes. *Random* and *purposeless* are hardly the words to apply to the Creator's order for each to reproduce "after its kind."

Furthermore, the commonly used term "natural selection" is so often personified that it has become a de facto "intelligent designer" (lower case intended). Natural selection is said to "operate on," "choose," "favor," and "provide"—all terms associated with intelligent decisions, none of which is present in unguided nature. The very term "selection" is both deceptive on the one hand and purposely kept in the story on the other because it gives to randomness the character of an overarching deity which/who can "fulfill" the "needs" of the planet.

None of this is empirical science, of course, but rather fanciful and sophisticated storytelling. If true, the biblical account of creation can be jettisoned. What is *observed*, what is *known*, is that natural processes are at best conservative (they keep things stable) and that life, order, and information deteriorate over time and eventually cease to exist.

Animals do adapt, but that adaptation ability is within the reproductive "seed" of that which exists. The "kind" surely does have the information necessary within the gene pool to adapt to environmental conditions. Plant and animal breeders take advantage of this phenomenon all the time, but they use the information already available in the plant or animal (the DNA), and then the breeder—an intelligent human—selects the characteristics that *he* desires. Natural processes do not "select" anything.

∽ 4 ∽

DAY FOUR

> Then God said, "Let there be lights in the firmament of the heavens to divide the day from the night; and let them be for signs and seasons, and for days and years; and let them be for lights in the firmament of the heavens to give light on the earth"; and it was so. Then God made two great lights: the greater light to rule the day, and the lesser light to rule the night. He made the stars also. God set them in the firmament of the heavens to give light on the earth, and to rule over the day and over the night, and to divide the light from the darkness. And God saw that it was good. So the evening and the morning were the fourth day. (Genesis 1:14-19)

Now that the planet had been properly prepared, the earth was ready for its clocks. The space-matter-time universe had been created. The shield of "waters" had been put in place somewhere above the "heaven," and the earth itself had been developed with seas and lands and "food" for the living creatures that were coming. Although there was some "light" that streamed into the creation, and the dark was divided from the light in an "evening and morning" cycle, there was no way for the future inhabitants to understand the successive passage of time.

Thus, there must be a time-keeping system for "signs and seasons, and for days and years."

The Lights of Heaven

There is a play on words in the Hebrew text that is easy to miss with any translation. God describes the reason for His action: "Let them be for *lights* in the firmament of the heavens to give *light* on the earth." The word translated "lights" is *ma'owr*. The second term is *'owr*. Obviously, the terms are related, but they do have a significantly different application.

Ma'owr is used to represent the light-holders, or light-bearers. *'Owr* defines the essence of light itself—light energy, we might say; or perhaps, visible light. The "light-holders" of Day Four are the "luminaries" (*ma'owr*) that carry or give off the "light" (*'owr*) that we see.

Perhaps a few references using *ma'owr* will help illustrate how the term is used.

- Exodus 13:21 – "a pillar of fire to give them *light*"
- Leviticus 24:2 – "pure oil of pressed olives for the *light*"
- Numbers 4:9 – "the lampstand of the *light*"
- Psalm 74:16 – "You have prepared the *light* and the sun"
- Ezekiel 32:8 – "all the bright *lights* of the heavens"

In each of these references, "light" refers to the ability to hold or contain the "light" that enables us to see. The Lord specifically said of the sun and the moon that they were to "to give light on the earth." God "made" these light-holders (as distinct from "created"). Apparently, God encapsulated the "light" of Day One into several different kinds of "luminaries" (see 1 Corinthians 15:41) and gave them the responsibility to "rule" the day and the night—and to set up a recognizable and reliable system for "signs and seasons, and for days and years."

For Signs

When describing the purpose for these "luminaries" of the heavens, God indicates they are to be for "signs." The English word is sometimes used for a miraculous event or some observable sequence that foretells a coming event. In this case, the Hebrew word (*'owth*) is not normally used that way. Usually, *'owth* speaks of a "mark" or a "token" that identifies rather than foretells. A few references may help understand how God uses the term.

- Genesis 4:15 – "The LORD set a *mark* on Cain."

- Genesis 9:13 – "I set My rainbow in the cloud, and it shall be for the *sign* of the covenant between Me and the earth."

- Genesis 17:11 – "You shall be circumcised in the flesh of your foreskins, and it shall be a *sign* of the covenant between Me and you."

- Exodus 10:2 – "That you may tell…the mighty things I have done in Egypt, and My *signs* which I have done among them, that you may know that I am the LORD."

- Exodus 12:13 – "The blood shall be a *sign* for you on the houses."

- Exodus 31:17 – "Observe the Sabbath….It is a *sign* between Me and the children of Israel forever."

- Isaiah 7:14 – "Therefore the Lord Himself will give you a *sign*: Behold, the virgin shall conceive and bear a Son, and shall call His name Immanuel."

Many more references could be cited, but these should suffice to illustrate that the lights in the heavens were never intended to be some sort of astrological sign (miracle, foretelling). Nor was there ever any hint that these majestic "rulers" of the heavens were to be worshiped. The horrible rebellion of ancient Babel under Nimrod (Genesis 10–11) fell into that trap. The nation of Israel repeatedly "served other gods, and worshiped them, either the sun or moon or any of the host of heaven" (Deuteronomy 17:3).

No, these great lights in the heavens were to serve as "marks" of the passage of time.

For Seasons

In addition to their role as markers for the passage of time, these lights were also to serve for "seasons." Again, the word choice is significant. The Hebrew term is *mow'ed* and specifies an appointed time. Here are a few references where *mow'ed* is used:

- Genesis 17:21 – "I establish with Isaac, whom Sarah shall bear to you at this *set time* next year."
- Exodus 23:15 – "You shall eat unleavened bread seven days, as I commanded you, at the *time appointed* in the month of Abib."
- Jeremiah 8:7 – "The stork in the heavens knows her *appointed times.*"
- Hosea 2:9 – "Take away my grain in its time and my new wine in its *season.*"

As God placed these luminaries in the heavens, He designed them as "identifiers" of time passage, but He also orchestrated their design and function so that they would identify specifically appointed events during time. The most obvious is the time of the Messiah and the fulfillment of all the prophetic promises of history.

> But when the fullness of the time had come, God sent forth His Son, born of a woman, born under the law, to redeem those who were under the law, that we might receive the adoption as sons. (Galatians 4:4-5)

> Now after Jesus was born in Bethlehem of Judea in the days of Herod the king, behold, wise men from the East came to Jerusalem, saying, "Where is He who has been born King of the Jews? For we have seen His star in the East and have come to worship Him." (Matthew 2:1-2)

Although this discussion is not about the miraculous incarnation of our Lord Jesus—the Word made flesh—that event was "appointed" in the design of the Creator and was so significant that the "markers" of heaven provided a visible testimony of that appointment!

But the ordinary role of these lights in the heavens is far more common. So common, in fact, that we seldom give it much thought. "He appointed the moon for seasons; The sun knows its going down" (Psalm 104:19). Every passing day, every passing month, each turn of the seasons, we simply say, "That's the way it is," and other than an occasional grumble about changes in the weather, we ignore the marvelous stability of our planet's appointments.

Indeed, we know that earth is orbiting the sun and that her rotational cycle lets us experience the "evening and the morning." But we see and speak of the "sunset" and the "sunrise." We understand that the moon regulates the tides of our oceans, but we rarely give the Creator credit for appointing the moon to "rule" in that way. Science has begun to grasp the significance of the precise tilt of earth on her axis that provides the energy disbursement mechanism that enables the "seasons." But how often do we remember that the Creator promised, "While the earth remains, Seedtime and harvest, Cold and heat, Winter and summer, And day and night Shall not cease" (Genesis 8:22)?

For Days and Years

And therein lies the basic, everyday value of the lights in the heavens. Without them, especially without the sun to rule the day and the moon to rule the night, we would not be able to maintain any kind of schedule or orderly progress.

The Hebrew word translated "rule" is *memshalah*. This term speaks of a realm or a ruler. It is very different from the commands to "subdue" and "have dominion," terms that were used to describe the stewardship authority given to mankind (Genesis 1:26, 28). The sun and the moon were to "have a realm of authority" defined by the Creator. The sun "presides" over the "day," and the moon "oversees" the "night." Neither one of them subdues or has dominion because man is the delegated authority to rule the earth. Yet both of them clearly "preside" in their spheres of authority. No "normal" life would be possible without their continual and faithful function.

Suppose that God had merely left the "light" of the first day beaming down from someplace outside the edge of the universe. We would have the "evening and morning" that existed from the beginning of Day One, but we would have no clear reference, no observable means of identifying the passage of time. Yes, there would be light and dark cycles, but no points to refer to, no phases of seasonal recognition, no "clock" to mark the greater spans of time.

The events of the fourth day were very important.

He Made the Stars Also

The Bible reveals that there are enormous numbers of stars (Hebrews 11:12), and that they are all "named" by their Creator (Psalm 147:4) and are part of the "signs" (tokens) of the heavens (Genesis 1:14-16). Evidently, they are to be both visible and identifiable. They are definitely not randomly scattered throughout space.

And each of the multiplied billions and billions of named stars has order, purpose, and identifying roles to play. When God spoke to Job, He insisted that Job ought to be able to observe the specified order in Pleiades and Orion, and that the seasonal changes in the "Mazzaroth" (the twelve divisions) were common knowledge, as well as the easily recognized "ordinances of heaven" (Job 38:31-33).

Not one of these uncountable stellar "lights" was developed over eons of time. "By the word of the LORD the heavens were made, and all the host of them by the breath of His mouth....For He spoke, and it was done; He commanded, and it stood fast" (Psalm 33:6, 9).

∽ 5 ∽
DAY FIVE

Then God said, "Let the waters abound with an abundance
of living creatures, and let birds fly above the earth across
the face of the firmament of the heavens." So God created
great sea creatures and every living thing that moves, with
which the waters abounded, according to their kind, and
every winged bird according to its kind. And God saw that
it was good. And God blessed them, saying, "Be fruitful and
multiply, and fill the waters in the seas, and let birds multiply on the earth." So the evening and the morning were the
fifth day. (Genesis 1:20-23)

The active verb in this passage is *bārā'*, or "create." Life is much more
than merely a collection of complex molecules. Up until this moment,
God had been organizing and structuring the "heavens and the earth"
so that the entire cosmos would be sufficient to sustain the life that He
would create on Days Five and Six.

As a reminder, the text of Genesis 1 uses the verb *bārā'* only on Days
One, Five, and Six. Days Two, Three, and Four are days of organizing
and structuring, along with the specialized "sprouting" of the earth-dirt
on Day Three. Apparently, God also "formed" the bodies of the air and
land creatures as He gave personal attention to the various "kinds" that
over the millennia to come would reveal something about Him.

Genesis 2:19 – Out of the ground the LORD God formed every beast of the field and every bird of the air, and brought them to Adam to see what he would call them.

Job 12:7 – But ask now the beasts, and they will teach you; and the birds of the air, and they will tell you.

Whatever God did and however God "made" and "formed" the animals, He made sure that we would understand that "creation" was the difference between the living creatures and the food that had "sprouted" for them to eat. These creatures were alive!

Designed to Fly

All of us have marveled at the birds of our world. Some are exquisitely brilliant in color, some sing so wonderfully that our hearts weep with joy, others glide and soar like the most graceful acrobats and ballet dancers. The lure of flight has driven many to experiment—from Icarus of Greek mythology to the Wright brothers. Yet all of our engineering skill, fighter jets, rockets, and commercial aircraft fail miserably to mimic the efficient and effective design of the tiniest bird.

Feathers

Feathers are not simple. They vary in type and use from the soft inner down to the varied wing, tail, and head crests. Feathers have shafts, veins, and barrels. They have colored pigments that vary across the spectrum, as well as various types of built-in prism designs that refract light.

Despite false reports of feathered dinosaurs, only birds have feathers. There are flightless birds with feathers (penguins, ostriches, etc.), but they are still birds. No evolutionist has a clue how feathers could have begun to develop. Indeed, there have been countless papers written on how such a thing *might have* come about, but none with observational, empirical data. Most naturalists attribute the origin of feathers to "natural selection," and they explain this process using magic words like "arose," "emerged," "appeared," "gave rise to," "derived," "modified," "burst onto the scene," "manufactured itself," and my favorite, "lucky."

Feathers are marvelously designed components. Everything we know and observe is that feathers were designed for the functions that they fulfill. Nothing in the observable world gives any evidence of "developing" feathers. There is no kind of fossil that shows some creature's skin developing sticks that turn into quills that turn into feathers. Feathers came into existence at the same time birds did.

Functions

Not all flying creatures are or were birds. There were some now-extinct flying reptiles like the pterosaur and *Pteranodon*, and there are modern bats (mammals). These do not have feathers, but they are obviously designed for flying.

All flying creatures are built around a skeleton that is light and composed mostly of hollow bones. This is very different from animals designed to walk on solid ground. These flying animals (birds, flying reptiles, bats) were *specifically designed* to fly. Their structure is different. Their activity is different. Their lifestyle is different.

The sternum (breastbone) of flying creatures is designed like the keel of a boat. This is the anchor point where most of the flight muscles are attached. Other air-breathing animals have nothing like this. In fact, things that fly have fewer bones than other mammals or reptiles—many of their bones are fused, making the overall skeleton rigid (sort of like the "unibody" of modern automobiles).

Neck vertebrae are also different in flying animals. Most flying creatures have to keep up the maintenance on their wings and bodies and need very flexible necks. Even the "wishbone" that we save at holiday dinners is unique to creatures that fly. Those rigid bones, keel-like sternum, and fused wishbone seem to have a clear purpose to help them fly.

Those of us who walk on the surface of the earth have lungs that act like bellows, pumping air in and out; our whole muscle and skeleton design is built around that function. In fact, we mix the "bad" air with the "good" in our lungs, mainly because we don't require as much oxygen for our normal functions.

Birds' lungs, however, are like tubes. These air sacs take in air at one end and expel it at the other (sort of like the grill-to-muffler system of a modern car). They are designed to take a unidirectional flow of air as the animal is flying. That design allows for a higher oxygen absorption by the blood when the muscles are working their hardest during flight.

The evidence demonstrates that flying creatures were designed to fly. Everything we observe in current fauna and in fossils supports the conclusion that they were created as flying creatures, just as Genesis teaches.

Designed to Swim

Water-based life is the only category singled out for survival (by omission) from the great judgment of the global Flood. Evidently, when God created the air and water creatures on Day Five, He paid some particular attention to an "abundance" of life that would "fill the waters in the seas" (Genesis 1:22).

Much of what we call "life" lives in the oceans, lakes, and rivers of our planet. Most of us know that the oceans cover over 70 percent of earth's surface, but what is often not understood is that the habitable volume for sea life is nearly 300 times more than the area that is available for land animals. Some oceans and lakes are actually very deep!

There are approximately 30,000 different species of land animals. That's about the same number as the diverse species of fish. But when you add in the rest of the various water-based living things, the number jumps to well over 200,000. Those water creatures, plus the nearly 10,000 species of birds, make Day Five a really busy day. God was not using hyperbole when He said, "Let the waters abound with an abundance of living creatures" (Genesis 1:20).

Gills

The capture of necessary oxygen under water is a very different process from that used by birds (tube-like lungs) or land animals (bellows-like lungs). Fish and many marine invertebrates "rake" in oxygen from water flowing through gills. When a fish (or a clam) opens its mouth, it sucks water into and past a system of filters that sift out debris. Once past these filters, the water passes over the gills.

Gills are amazing, multifaceted devices! Boney pieces that hang in the middle of the fish's mouth support very thin filaments called lamellae that collect the oxygen. Within the lamellae are numerous capillaries that exchange the oxygen for carbon dioxide. The oxygen goes into the bloodstream and the carbon dioxide goes back out into the water. Clever, yes?

Actually, this is not only clever, but absolutely necessary. Water contains less than 5 percent of the oxygen that is available in air, so gills have to work more efficiently than lungs. Scientists have discovered that gills are able to get about 85 percent of the available oxygen out of the water that flows through and over them. That is much better than humans can do with our lungs. Furthermore, if we had gills like fish, we could not survive on land. Gills require the buoyancy of water to function.

Many water creatures don't have gills. Starfish breathe through their feet and through small breathing tubes distributed all over their bodies. Marine worms (there are lots of them) breathe through their skin. Everything that lives in the water is designed to function in water—with just the right equipment to make life work. Even the air-breathing marine mammals—like whales, porpoises, seals, and walruses—have specialized nostrils, lungs, muscles, and other equipment to function best in water.

It's hard to imagine how any of these creatures could have just "happened."

Scales, Skin, and Crusty Stuff

The oceans, lakes, and rivers of our world are full of amazingly different forms of life. Just as gills and other forms of oxygen-gathering organs differ widely by body type, environment, and lifestyle, so do outer coverings. Scales are common enough, but there are vast differences among scaly creatures.

Some scales are really big (two to three inches across). Some are microscopic and feel like slick skin, but are still scales. There are scales made out of bone, out of dentin (cosmine), and out of cartilage. Some scales have razor-sharp ridges down the center or on the sides. Others are flat, curved, rounded, or elongated. There are lots of different kinds of scales.

Many creatures living in the water have skin, such as the octopus, squid, and cuttlefish. Others, like eels and lampreys, are less known specifically for their coverings, but wild stories abound about their terrible teeth. Then there are the Batoidea (which include electric rays, butterfly rays, round rays, manta rays, guitarfish, and sawfish)—nearly 500 different kinds of these flat-bodied, wing-shape animals—all of which have skin rather than scales.

Some of these skin-covered creatures (like squids and cuttlefish) have *chromatrophores* in their skin that enable them to change colors quickly (like a chameleon) to mimic their environmental surroundings. Most of the time, the color changes vary to blend in from side-to-side and top-to-bottom, making the animal nearly invisible from every viewpoint. Sometimes these color patterns are flashed back and forth in mating dances.

The mechanics of this color-changing ability are amazing! Groups of red, yellow, brown, and black pigments are perched above a layer of reflective cells that actually can be oriented in different directions to refract light into different colors. Coordinated muscles "squish" the cells in just the right sequence to produce the right combination of colors to match the surrounding area. The pigments and the refraction capabilities are sometimes coupled with chemical reactions that produce, essentially, an infinite spectrum of colors—roughly equivalent to 360 dots per square inch (dpi) on a TV screen or a printed page.

There are numerous evolutionary explanations offered for how this remarkable ability came about, but those stories make Disney Imagineers look like kids drawing stick men. The biblical record makes a much more believable story. The observable facts demonstrate that these remarkable animals were created that way.

Thousands of water creatures have external skeletons. No scales, no skin, just hard crusty stuff on the outside. These are not simple creatures. How did they just "happen"?

The marine invertebrates comprise most of the so-called Cambrian Explosion of life. Starfish, jellyfish, coral, trilobites, worms, sea cucumbers, etc., just "appeared" in the fossil record—fully formed, just like they are today. And except for the extinct forms, which also appeared in the fossil record fully formed, they all perfectly fit and happily function in their modern environments—as though they were designed to be there.

Sea Monsters

In Genesis 1:21, the King James Version of the Bible translates the Hebrew word *tanniym* as "whales." That leads to an unfortunate misunderstanding in the reader's mind, since the word is elsewhere translated "dragon," "serpent," or "monster," as it should be.

The fossil record contains some rather startling bones of huge marine dinosaurs. Several types of extinct plesiosaur are known. The *Elasmosaurus* (long neck) and *Kronosaurus* were about 50 feet long and are among the more famous. Their fossil bones fit the description of "sea monster" pretty well. Then there are mosasaurs, which ranged in size from 10 to 50 feet. The Institute for Creation Research has a mosasaur skull in its collection that is about 4.5 feet long and nearly 3 feet wide. The skull has segregated jaws and double rows of teeth. Sea monster, indeed!

Any one of these fossils could have been the ancestor of the living leviathan that God Himself describes to Job during their discourse in Job 38–41. One land dinosaur and one marine dinosaur were certainly alive at the time of Job, who was a contemporary of Abraham. Note God's description of the "sea monster."

> "Who can open the doors of his face, With his terrible teeth all around? His rows of scales are his pride, Shut up tightly as with a seal; One is so near another That no air can come between them; They are joined one to another, They stick together and cannot be parted.

> "His sneezings flash forth light, And his eyes are like the eyelids of the morning. Out of his mouth go burning lights; Sparks of fire shoot out. Smoke goes out of his nostrils, As from a boiling pot and burning rushes. His breath kindles coals, And a flame goes out of his mouth.

> "Strength dwells in his neck, And sorrow dances before him. The folds of his flesh are joined together; They are firm on him and cannot be moved. His heart is as hard as stone, Even as hard as the lower millstone. When he raises himself up, the mighty are afraid; Because of his crashings they are beside themselves.

"Though the sword reaches him, it cannot avail; Nor does spear, dart, or javelin. He regards iron as straw, And bronze as rotten wood. The arrow cannot make him flee; Sling-stones become like stubble to him. Darts are regarded as straw; He laughs at the threat of javelins. His undersides are like sharp potsherds; He spreads pointed marks in the mire.

"He makes the deep boil like a pot; He makes the sea like a pot of ointment. He leaves a shining wake behind him; One would think the deep had white hair.

"On earth there is nothing like him, Which is made without fear. He beholds every high thing; He is king over all the children of pride." (Job 41:14-34)

If modern scholars are right and this creature is nothing more than a crocodile, then God is confused about what He created. The words of the biblical text do not describe a crocodile. The awesome marine creature described by God to Job is much different from any animal about which we have current knowledge.

It is remarkable that every culture, from just about every recorded era, has stories about sea monsters. Some of them are pretty wild, but as recently as 1934 several newspapers recorded the finding of a 30-foot-long "sea monster" washed up on the beach south of Henry Island in British Columbia. A Japanese sea trawler caught a long-dead sea creature in its nets off the coast of New Zealand in 1974 that looked suspiciously like a plesiosaur, although it was too decayed to make a positive identification. And surely news and speculation about creatures like the Loch Ness Monster have not escaped notice. While these stories do not prove the existence of sea monsters, there are similarities that run through many of the accounts that often match elements of what God described to Job.

Everywhere one can look, from the soaring birds to the scary ptero-dactyls, from the sea monster to the sea cucumber, the design, purpose, complex construction, environmental fit, awesome beauty, and instant camouflage of these creatures all display and demonstrate the majestic wonder of God's fifth day of creation.

∾ 6 ∾
DAY SIX

Then God said, "Let the earth bring forth the living creature according to its kind: cattle and creeping thing and beast of the earth, each according to its kind"; and it was so. And God made the beast of the earth according to its kind, cattle according to its kind, and everything that creeps on the earth according to its kind. And God saw that it was good. (Genesis 1:24-25)

Continuing to create and make the living creatures, God turned His attention to the land.

Cattle

The Hebrew term *behemah* is used by the Creator and later by Moses to describe the land animals that people were most familiar with. "Cattle" still generally means any kind of livestock, from cows to sheep. Most of the 189 times the term appears in the Old Testament, the context references food or sacrificial laws. (Obviously, the reference to food was made long *after* permission was given to Noah in Genesis 9:3 to eat animal flesh.)

Whatever these animals were, it appears clear that they would have included all of the land animals that mankind has generally domesticated or raised agriculturally for food. The main difference between these "cattle" and the "beasts of the earth" seems to be their personality preference. Animals express self-awareness as well as distinct personalities. Some, of course, are less personable than others, but there is an obvious gap between farm animals and house pets and the "wild beasts" of our planet.

Just what separates the "fowls" that fly in the atmosphere of Day Five (most of which feed and house on land) and the "cattle" of Day Six is not clear either in biology or in Scripture. God separated them in His mind, however, and as any person who has had close contact with animals knows, farm animals and house pets are generally given far more freedom than birds. Birds generally need a cage or a chain or they will fly away. Cats and dogs, however, know the hand that feeds them, and often "manage" the people who care for them!

Creeping Things

A second broad term used by the Creator to designate a category of animals is the Hebrew word *remes*. This is used mostly in the creation record, the account of the global Flood, and the dietary laws. Twice the word appears in the Psalms, and once in a prophetic passage. All of the occasions appear to speak of smaller animals that "slink" or "glide" in the more inaccessible parts of the earth.

The man-made system of taxonomy, as useful as it may be for our efforts to categorize, doesn't seem to apply here. God uses much broader concepts, evidently creating the vast "kinds" in direct proportion to how these creatures would relate to humans. Thus, "cattle" would be the types of animals that would be more easily brought into association with mankind. "Creeping things" and "beasts of the earth" are broad summaries of animal life that would not normally be part of a domesticated household.

Therefore, it seems appropriate to think of these "creeping things" as the weasels, rodents, possums, shrews, reptiles, amphibians, etc. That list is in no sense meant to be complete, but merely illustrative, since there are nearly 20,000 different species of those kinds of "creeping things." The list would probably also include the 1,000,000 or so species of insects and the 100,000 or so species of spiders and scorpions. People don't generally get along with any of those.

Beasts of the Earth

This final category obviously includes everything that is not "cattle" or "creeping thing." That phrase appears 24 times in the Old Testament. In most of the places it appears outside of the creation account, it describes the beasts eating other animals—and in some cases, the flesh of wicked men. Whatever these animals are, they are not pets!

When God gives His discourse to Job, He mentions the lion, the wild goat, the wild ass, and the ostrich as examples of the types of animals that Job or his fellow men would not keep around their houses or their fields. God also takes special care to describe "behemoth" and "leviathan"—both of which are huge, wild animals Job was familiar with but would not plan to keep as pets.

Leviathan is obviously a "sea monster" that has evidently become extinct. Behemoth fits perfectly the description of the larger sauropods (four-footed dinosaurs) that we find in the fossil record.

> "Look now at the behemoth, which I made along with you; He eats grass like an ox. See now, his strength is in his hips, And his power is in his stomach muscles.

> "He moves his tail like a cedar; The sinews of his thighs are tightly knit. His bones are like beams of bronze, His ribs like bars of iron.

> "He is the first of the ways of God; Only He who made him can bring near His sword.

> "Surely the mountains yield food for him, And all the beasts of the field play there. He lies under the lotus trees, In a covert of reeds and marsh. The lotus trees cover him with their shade; The willows by the brook surround him. Indeed the river may rage, Yet he is not disturbed; He is confident, though the Jordan gushes into his mouth, Though he takes it in his eyes, Or one pierces his nose with a snare." (Job 40:15-24)

Many modern Bible editions attempt to pass this creature off as either an elephant or a hippopotamus. Once again, either God was confused about what He and Job were both familiar with or the scholars are wrong. Neither an elephant nor a hippopotamus has a tail, for instance, like a cedar tree. And although the hippopotamus lives in a river, the elephant does not. An elephant may live near mountains and under trees, but the hippopotamus does not. But the total description is easily matched to what we know from the fossil record.

After Its Kind

All of the replicating processes God created, from the simplest plant to the most complex life, were limited to reproducing "after its kind." This emphasis is repeated on Day Three to the "sprouts" of earth, and on Days Five and Six to all of the living creatures. Everything was to "fill the earth" and be "fruitful"—but only "after its kind."

The design implications are vital to understand. Not only do the obvious limitations prohibit the atheistic concept of a "common ancestor," but the inferences certainly seem to be verified by observation. That is, within each kind is the design power to adapt quickly to environmental changes that will permit the kind to propagate itself over time.

Human efforts to categorize differences between species are just that—human efforts. Mankind is just now scratching the surface of the enormously complex DNA instructions that reside in the "seed" of everything that reproduces. As more is unraveled (literally) and documented, scholars are becoming aware that the so-called "junk DNA" is clearly *not* junk! Perhaps we will never fully understand what our Creator produced in the "seed" of plants and animals, but it is quite clear that nature doesn't select anything. The power to adapt resides within the organism.

The Image of God

> Then God said, "Let Us make man in Our image, according to Our likeness; let them have dominion over the fish of the sea, over the birds of the air, and over the cattle, over all the earth and over every creeping thing that creeps on the earth." So God created man in His own image; in the image of God He created him; male and female He created them. (Genesis 1:26-27)

Theologians and students of Scripture have been pondering this passage for millennia. Just what is it that God "created" in His own "image"? Just what *is* God's image? There are a number of hints in the Bible, but not enough to be completely sure; some things remain secret with God (Deuteronomy 29:29).

The man and the woman—each of whom was specially created in God's own image—were vastly different from the rest of the living creatures. While we share the "life" of other living animals, our bodies are enormously more versatile and capable than other living things. Human emotion expresses a vast range of feelings and reactions that no animal shares. Intellectually, the human brain far exceeds any animal brain in capacity and ability. While all creation will one day acknowledge the Creator, it is only man who now joyfully worships or consciously rebels.

Only One of Each

When the Creator determined to "make" man, He made only one male and one female. All of the other living animals in the air, in the water, on and under the earth, were made at least in the hundreds of pairs, if not thousands or millions. They were "abundant" and "filled" the air, sea, and land.

Not so with Adam and Eve.

> And the LORD God formed man of the dust of the ground, and breathed into his nostrils the breath of life; and man became a living being....And the LORD God caused a deep sleep to fall on Adam, and he slept; and He took one of his ribs, and closed up the flesh in its place. Then the rib which the LORD God had taken from man He made into a woman, and He brought her to the man. (Genesis 2:7, 21-22)

Please notice the precise language used about the "forming" of Adam and the "making" of Eve. The Holy Spirit specifically used the Hebrew word *yatsar* to describe the formation of Adam's body. As was discussed earlier, *yatsar* is a "hands-on" verb used to describe personal involvement. This was the "first man" (1 Corinthians 15:47), who was unique from everything else that had been made.

Then, the Creator took some "rib" from Adam and "made" a woman. The English translations don't quite do justice to the record. *Tesla* is the Hebrew word used, and every other time it appears in the Bible, it is translated "side." Surely what God took from Adam would have included a rib, but there was muscle and other tissue as well, which is why Adam later said: "This is now bone of my bones and flesh of my flesh; She shall be called Woman, Because she was taken out of Man" (Genesis 2:23).

In both cases, with the handful of dirt and the piece of Adam's side, God "formed" and "made" the independent and unique bodies of Adam and Eve.

The Genesis Mandate

> Then God blessed them, and God said to them, "Be fruitful and multiply; fill the earth and subdue it; have dominion over the fish of the sea, over the birds of the air, and over every living thing that moves on the earth." (Genesis 1:28)

Part of the difference of being made in God's image was the unique responsibility of stewardship given to humanity in Genesis 1:28. Essentially, this text sets the stage for the responsibility that all of humanity would carry as long as earth endures. This stewardship has never been withdrawn or abrogated in any way, except to be somewhat extended and subrogated to collective humanity after the great Flood.

Be Fruitful and Multiply

There is more to this command than "Have lots of kids." Obviously, both the terms used and the phrase itself imply reproduction, but if all this command signifies is to "breed" prolifically, then there is not much to it.

It is clear that God intended for mankind to take the responsibility of "multiplying" far more seriously than merely having large families. The pressure to protect and direct the next generation is a God-placed concept in all living creatures—especially among humans. That "instinct" to be fruitful and multiply is the fountainhead from which the rest of the Genesis mandate flows.

Fill the Earth

The Hebrew *male'* is broadly used in the nearly 300 times it is found in the Old Testament. It is used to describe "filling" a space, as when locusts filled the Egyptians' houses during the Ten Plagues (Exodus 10:6). It sometimes identifies the completion of a specific time, like when the seven days were "fulfilled" after the Lord turned the Nile into blood (Exodus 7:25). But many of the passages deal with the "completing" or "fulfilling" of promises and prophecies.

Whatever may have been delegated to humanity (and to animals) in the authorization to "fill" the earth, it is certainly clear that God has "arranged" (if that is the proper word) for His creation to "fulfill" His plans—even though many (both men and animals) do their best to thwart those plans. The capacity to "fill" would involve at least the following abilities:

- Frequent and successful reproduction "after its kind"
- Early maturity and long fertility potential
- Informational capacity (DNA) within the "kind" to adapt to new environments
- Intellectual capacity to plan for and protect successful "filling"
- Geometric growth patterns that stabilize generations and communities

Subdue the Earth

The Hebrew word *kabash* is only used 15 times in the Old Testament, but it always carries the idea of bringing something into or under subjection. Obviously, when the Creator issued the authority to Adam and to Eve to "subdue" the earth, God was not giving an order that would be easily carried out. Mankind would have to learn about earth's systems and processes, organize and utilize that knowledge in productive ways to benefit others and honor the Creator, disseminate the information gained and distribute the products to everyone, and receive and detail the divine evaluation ("very good").

Have Dominion

The Hebrew word *radah* is used 27 times in the Old Testament, always having the basic meaning of "rule." It can be used in the sense of an evil rule, even a rule with "force and cruelty" (Ezekiel 34:4), but that idea is not inherent in the word. The ruler determines the kind of rule, not the authority itself. The *way* one rules is determined by the character of the one who rules.

When the Creator granted the authority to "subdue" (conquer) and to "have dominion" (rule), He had just brought into existence His "image" (man) who would share regency with Him over the earth in its pristine condition. Those stewards would soon rebel against God's ownership and distort the authority that had been granted (Genesis 3). What has happened subsequent to that rebellion, however, in no way abrogates the design and purpose of His "good" mandate.

What Happened to God's "Very Good" World?

> And God said, "See, I have given you every herb that yields seed which is on the face of all the earth, and every tree whose fruit yields seed; to you it shall be for food. Also, to every beast of the earth, to every bird of the air, and to everything that creeps on the earth, in which there is life, I have given every green herb for food"; and it was so. Then God saw everything that He had made, and indeed it was very good. So the evening and the morning were the sixth day. (Genesis 1:29-31)

At the end of God's creative activities, He surveyed His work and pronounced it "very good." Coming from the holy and omniscient Creator, this can only mean that everything He had created demonstrated flawless perfection. But the world of corruption and death in which we now live cannot be described that way. What led to this drastic change?

Genesis 2 describes how God prepared a special garden in which the man and the woman would begin their stewardship duties. There, He gave them a specific command—they could eat of every tree in the garden, "but the tree of the knowledge of good and evil you shall not eat, for in the day that you eat of it you shall surely die" (Genesis 2:17).

Genesis 3 relates the well-known story of the serpent's deception of Eve, her taking of the fruit and giving it to her husband, and Adam's willful decision to disobey God.

Because of their choices, the world and its inhabitants were cursed. An animal was killed to provide a covering for Adam and Eve's nakedness, and they were barred from the garden "lest he put out his hand and take also of the tree of life, and eat, and live forever" (Genesis 3:22) in a perpetual state of sin and decay.

Sin and death now dominate creation. Man has become separated from God and is born with a nature that will inevitably rebel against the Creator. Such a setting would be utter futility were it not for the prescient foreknowledge of the Creator displayed in the effort to redeem Adam and Eve from their doom. In the immediate actions of our Creator for Adam and Eve, you and I are encouraged to trust His later provision of "the Lamb slain from the foundation of the world" (Revelation 13:8). Over 4,000 years after sin's entry into the world, the Redeemer would come with the price necessary to buy all humanity back from death. Genesis 3 illustrates what God would do in the future, as well as what He did for humanity's immediate need.

EPILOGUE

If God—the One who could speak the universe into existence with a command—is indeed the Creator, then He is the Owner of all that exists. Man is, therefore, a steward and is ultimately accountable to the Owner for all that is done with life and resources. On the other hand, if matter has always existed and random forces have been inexorably evolving upward, then humans are simply the best organisms that have been produced so far, and man, by default, becomes the owner of all he can rule. There is no logical middle ground.

The physical universe and all the information that humanity can uncover will be interpreted in the light of the belief system or worldview each individual holds. To the naturalist, this life is all that there is. There is no future, no afterlife. When you're dead, you're dead!

Such hopeless beliefs drive many into lives of debauchery and hedonism, or fill the couches of psychologists and psychiatrists all over the world. There is no "good news" in the evolutionary theory.

There is, however, glorious wonder and life-changing power in the gospel presented in the Bible. That message of salvation describes an eternal conversion from a spiritually dead and physically dying existence to spiritual eternal life now and a totally flawless "new heavens and new earth" in which those who are so "saved" will become both immortal and holy. How can such a thing be? Such a salvation must have *power*:

- power to transform now, in this life (Romans 12:2)
- power to enrich our current condition (2 Corinthians 9:11)

- power to bring satisfying peace to all situations (Hebrews 13:20-21)
- power to change the mortal body into the immortal and everlasting being who will live eternally with the Creator (1 Corinthians 15: 53-54)

But (and this is the point of this book) upon what is the "power" of the Good News based? Perhaps one can long for the changes promised and the beauty of eternal life spoken of in the pages of the Bible, but how can one believe such intangible promises unless there is some demonstration of the power necessary to defeat death and create new life?

Such supernatural power was amply demonstrated in the six days of creation recorded in Genesis. God verifies, augments, describes, and cites His creative power without alteration throughout the Bible. Those words describe and present a Being whose power is limitless and whose knowledge is all-encompassing.

The Creator God of the Bible is our source for life, and our only means of redemption. Without Him, we are and have nothing. The Good News of salvation is inexorably rooted in what God did "in the beginning" during the six days of creation.